Psalms of Praise

CONCORDIA®

Selections from Psalms/Now
by Leslie Brandt

Concordia Publishing House, St. Louis, Missouri

ISBN 0-570-07453-3
MANUFACTURED IN THE UNITED STATES OF AMERICA

"God forgives all my sins;
He touches my afflictions with healing;
He snatches me back
from the gaping jaws of hell;
He covers me with concern and love."

Praising God is reciting what He has done for you, your family, your friends, your nation. God's love for His people is marvelous.

Praising God is reflecting God's acts of love with your own life. You shape God's image in the world.

Praising God is responding to His abiding interest in you. The psalmist marvels: "I am His delight and His heart's desire." Imagine!

When you read these translations from Leslie Brandt's Psalms/Now, they will become your words of praise to your loving and beloved God.

9

My heart overflows with gratitude to God.
I feel so exuberant
I simply must express or explode.
I will give voice to my exultations;
I will sing Your praises, O my God.

You helped me stand firm
in spite of those who had it in for me,
and they were not successful
in their efforts to discredit me.

You have destroyed great forces in history
    that rose up to oppose You.
You continue to rule over our fractured world,
    to sit in judgment over its nations and peoples.
You offer Your strong hand to those who are oppressed,
    Your loving concern to those who are troubled.
You never hide from those who seek You
    or forsake those who cling to You.

Sing the praises of God;
    proclaim loudly His deeds to the people.
For while He judges evildoers,
    He hears and remembers the cries of those in distress.

I need always Your gracious love.
You know all about my inner fears and doubts.
You hold me back from the brink of destruction.
You make it possible for me to sing Your praises
    and to rejoice in Your perpetual deliverance.
Ungodly nations sink in their own sewage.
Men who promote evil
        snare themselves in their own nets,
    but those who recognize their need of You
        shall be found by You.

Is it any wonder
    my heart overflows with gratitude to God?

18

It is no wonder that I love You, O God.
You have granted me a security
that I could never find
among the things of this world.

You have erased from my life the fear of death.
What follows the grave is not my fearful concern.
The traumatic experiences of this life
cannot destroy me.
You are never out of reach
but are ever aware of my problems and conflicts.

How great and all-powerful is my God!
The quaking of the earth,
the shaking of the mountains,
the blackness of the night,
the beauty of the heavens,
the lightning that crisscrosses our skies,
the oceans that lash against our shores:
this and much more bear witness
to the majesty of my God.
And this is the God who is concerned about me.
He reaches into my distraught life
to heal my wounds.
He encompasses me with eternal love.

He abides with me
even in the midst of conflict or calamity.
He sets me free from self-idolatry
so I may serve His creatures about me.
He shields me from the forces that are intent
on my destruction.
I am His delight and heart's desire.
It is no wonder, O God, that I love You.

Can there be any God but this God that I love?
He surrounds me with His strength
and clothes me with His grace.
He puts into my hands gifts to relay to others.
He entrusts me with tasks
far beyond my human abilities
and enables me to carry them out.
He ordains me as His son and servant
destined to accomplish His purposes
amongst the peoples of this world.

It is thus that I celebrate God's presence
in my life and world.
God is not dead; He lives.
I rejoice in His concern and love for me.
I will proclaim, O Lord,
Your praises to anyone who will listen to me.
I will sing and shout and dance
in the joy of knowing that You are my God.

21

O God,
in the grace and strength that You daily grant,
Your servant finds reason for celebration.
You have truly fulfilled his innermost longings.
You have responded to his deepest needs.

He asked for security,
and You encompassed him with love.
He looked to You for life,
and You granted him life eternal.
He sought for identity,
and You adopted him as Your son.
Whatever is of value and worth in his life

has come by way of Your rich blessings.
His heart is glad in the realization
of Your eternal presence.
He knows that he will never lose Your love.

I raise my voice in praise, O God,
because no one can separate me from You.
Though circumstances threaten me
and my own obsessions entangle me,
You will never let me go.
Your great power is sufficient to set me free
from these things that hurt my soul.
If I put my trust in You,
You will not allow them to destroy me.
I find so many reasons for praising You, O God.

48

How great is my God!
He soars above our poor intellects
like a snow-capped mountain
over a sun-baked desert.
He scatters the profound theories of wise men
like leaves pushed around by a winter wind.
He shatters
the assembled might of world governments
as an earthquake levels a city.
He reaches down in tenderness
to earth's poor creatures
and draws them to Himself.

Consider with me the greatness of my God.
Measure His judgments;
embrace His eternal love.
Stand tall in your faith
courageous in your commitment,
for He is truly a great God.

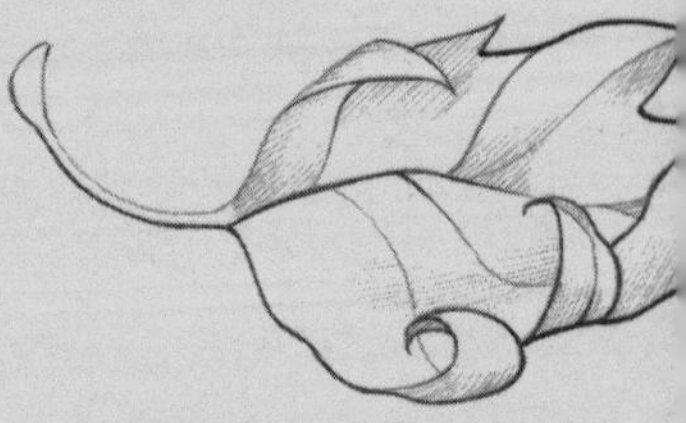

103

My heart is bursting with praises to God;
every fiber of my being reaches out in rejoicing!
How can I ever forget His many blessings?
He forgives all my sins;
He touches my afflictions with healing;
He snatches me back
from the gaping jaws of hell;
He covers me with concern and love;
He fulfills my deepest desires and gives me meaning for life and purpose for living.

God is a God of justice and judgment,
but He is on the side of those who need His help.
He is angry with those
who persistently rebel against Him,
but He pours out His love
upon those who turn to Him.
He does not give us our just deserts
or pay us what we well deserve.
He is grieved when we so miserably fail,
but He quickly draws us to His forgiving heart
and accepts us just as if it never happened.
He looks with tenderness
upon His faltering children;
He knows and understands our fallible natures.

Man by himself is a pitiful picture of weakness.
Now and then one will,
like a streaking meteor,
blaze out across the skies of time,
only to become a smoking cinder
at the end of his short journey.
But those who tie on
to God's loving will and purposes
become the objects
of His eternal mercy and righteousness.

Rejoice with me,
you who are His invisible servants
and you who hear and obey His voice.
Shout His praises,
you who are His children
and you who serve
as His ministers and priests.
There is no time for despair and discouragement.
Whoever and wherever you are,
lift your hearts in praises to God.

105

How great is my God,
and how I love to sing His praises!
Whereas I am often frightened
when I think about the future,
and confused and disturbed
by the rapidly changing events about me,
my heart is secured and made glad
when I remember how He has cared for me
throughout the past.

When I was brought forth from my mother's womb,
God's hand was upon me.
Through parents and people who cared,
He loved and sheltered me
and set me upon His course for my life.
Through illness and accident
my God has sustained me.
Around pitfalls and precipices
He has safely led me.
When I became rebellious
and struck out on my own,
He waited patiently for me to return.
When I fell on my face in weakness and failure,
He gently set me upon my feet again.
He did not always prevent me from hurting

myself,
but He took me back to heal my wounds.
Even out of the broken pieces of my defeats
He created a vessel of beauty and usefulness.

Through trials and errors, failures and successes,
my God has cared for me.
Form infancy to adulthood
He has never let me go.
His love has led me—or followed me—
through the valleys of sorrow
and the highlands of joy,
through times of want
and years of abundance.
He has bridged impassable rivers
and moved impossible mountains.
Sometimes through me,
sometimes in spite of me,
He seeks to accomplish His purposes in my
life.

He has kept me through the stormy past;
He will secure and guide me
through the perilous future.
I need never be afraid,
no matter how uncertain
the months or years ahead of me.
How great is my God,
and how I love to sing His praises!

III

My heart is full today.
I am so grateful
for all that God has done for me.
I need but crawl out of my corner
of depression and self-pity
and look around me to see
how great my God is.
I cannot see Him,
but I can see the works of His hands.
He is a merciful and loving God.
How tenderly He deals with those
whose hearts are open to Him!
He is a righteous and faithful God.
His promises and precepts are forever.
He is a majestic and powerful God.
He created me and sustains me day by day.
He is a forgiving God.
He takes me back to His loving heart
when I go astray.
He is in this world today.
And those who recognize and accept His presence
are building on foundations
that are eternally secure.
How grateful I am to my God today!

113

How great and glorious is our God!
From hour to hour, from day to day
our lives ought to overflow
with praise and gratitude.
It is amazing, even fantastic,
how our God permeates every facet of our lives
and can work out His purposes through them
despite our human faults and failures.

He creates beauty out of the dust
of our fallen natures.
Out of the ashes of our failures
He brings forth meaning and purpose.
He exalts the humble and enriches the poor.
He transforms our weaknesses
into channels of strength.
Our emptiness becomes
a vessel of His fullness,
our spiritual poverty
the basis for His eternal grace.
Our errors and mistakes
are stepping-stones to success.
Our defeats are but incidents
on the road to victory.

But this is God's doing, not ours.
How great and glorious is our God!

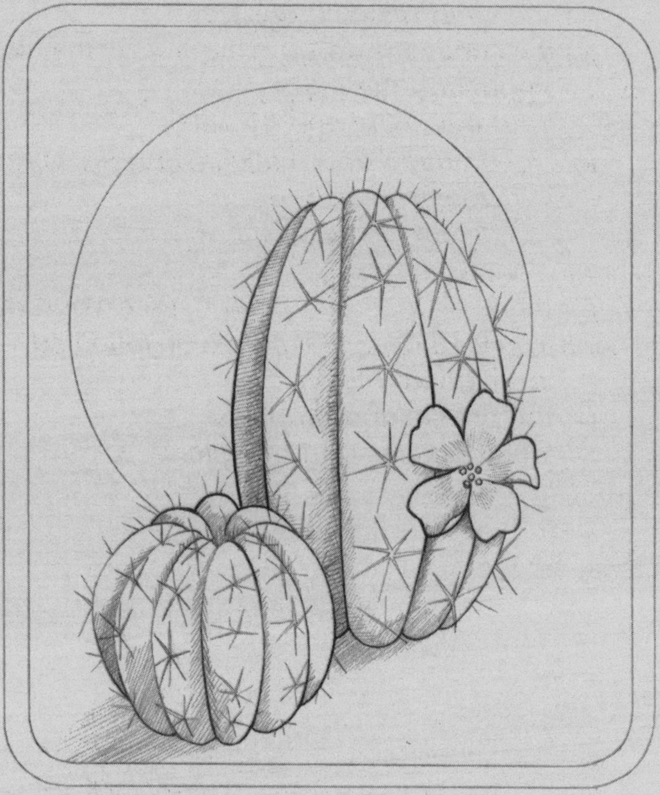

136

Thank You, God,
for all these things that reveal your love.
Thank You for the heavens that cover us,
for the earth beneath our feet,
for the sun in the day and the stars of the night,
for the snow and the rains
and the rivers and the lakes,
for mountains and valleys and trees and flowers.

Thank You, God,
for those people who demonstrate Your love.
Thank You for those great men who followed You throughout history,
for the priests and prophets
and apostles and ministers,

for doctors and teachers and mothers and fathers
and painters and musicians and writers
and farmers and laborers and clerks,
for those men and women who accepted Your love
and dedicated their lives
to loving their fellowman.

Thank You, God,
for choosing me to be one of Your people,
for calling me and equipping me to communicate
Your love to my world about me.
Thank You, God.

137

How grateful we are, O God,
for our great country
for the blessings You lavish upon our land!
How concerned we are, O God,
that our very nation may become our god
and that we worship the gifts
rather than the Giver!

Is it possible, O God,
that our laws may circumvent Your will?
that our freedom may place chains on others?
that our wealth impoverish someone?
that our power may come
by way of another's weakness?
that our enemies may be those
who are obedient to You?
Dare we pray, O God,
that You take away those things that come
between us and You?
that You raise up men who will oppose
those institutions and those citizens
who carelessly, even unconsciously,
equate patriotism with allegiance to You?

We do pray, O God,
that our nation be restored to Your objectives
and that Your children who abide in this land
dedicate their lives to You and Your
purposes.

138

I am exceedingly grateful, O Lord,
for You have heard my cries and complaints,
and You responded with mercy and strength.
Now my life is overflowing with thanksgiving,
and my mouth is filled with Your praises.

If only the leaders of our disjointed world
would listen to Your words
and direct their people in accord with Your will,
they would then know the meaning of peace,
and they would rejoice in the ways of God.

You have not shielded me
from the pains of trouble
or the ravages of conflict,
but You have kept me
even amid sorrow and suffering.
You take my side against the enemies of my soul,
and You will not allow them to destroy me.

Thus I know You will fulfill Your purpose for my life.
Your love and mercy is everlasting;
You will not let me go.

146

Praise God!
As long as I have breath in my body,
I will praise God!

Don't pin your hopes on the genius of man.
His ultimate end is the same as yours,
and he becomes once more
like the dust from which he came.

That person is secure
who draws his strength from God.
He who created the earth and all upon it,
He is He who can heal the wounds
and mend the fractures of our disjointed world.
He can break the bonds of obsession
and pierce man's stupor with visions of truth.
He tenderly reaches out
to those who are oppressed
and reveals His concern
for those who are lost and lonely.
He watches over His own
while the paths of the godless
lead to their own destruction.

This is the God who cannot die!
Praise God!
Amen!

147 - 150

How good it is to celebrate God's presence
and to sing His praises throughout each day!
We celebrate what He has done for man
through history:
His creation of our world
and the sun and the moon
and the unnumbered stars
that light up our universe;
His creatures that swim and crawl
and walk and fly upon our planet;
His children destined to enjoy
these great gifts about them.
We praise Him for dealing with creature man:
through His blessings heaped upon him;
His revelations through signs and wonders;
His tender love and gentle concern
in His caring for him.
We praise Him for His devoted servants:
who communicated His Word;
who performed His miracles;
who brought His healing to men's hurts.

We celebrate His continued blessings to our world:
the flowers that bloom in glorious color;
the rains that freshen the earth;
the birds that fill the air with song.
We give thanks for His perpetual love:
His forgiveness of men's sin;
His pursuit of those who run from Him;
His reaching out to heal them
and to draw them to Himself.

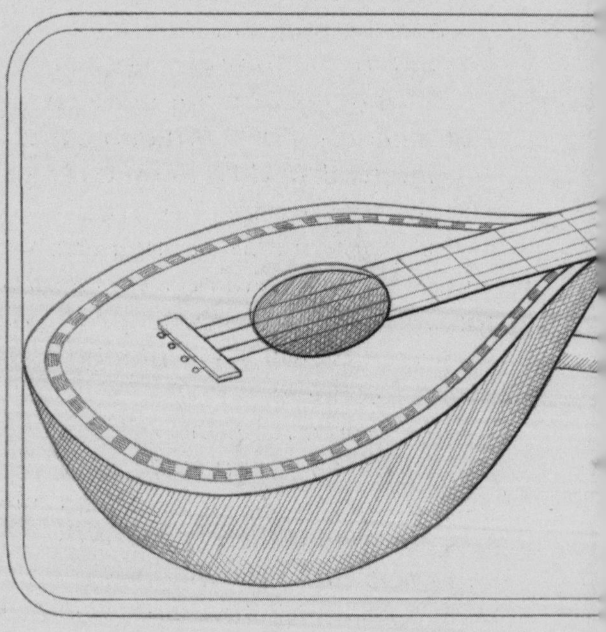

We call upon all men to praise the Lord:
those who preach to proclaim His love;
those who sing to glorify His name;
those who can shout or whistle
or write or paint
or dance or play musical instruments
or pound on drums or ring bells
to join in celebrating
the majesty of our great and loving God.

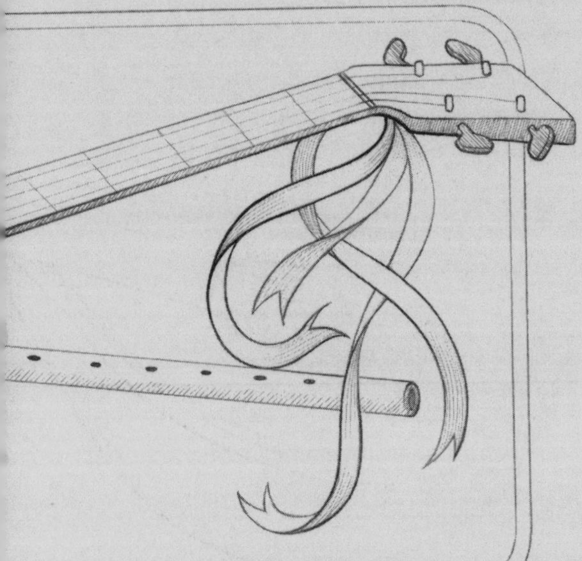